JEANNIE BAKER

The Story of Rosy Dock

Greenwillow Books, New York

To David and Haydn, Thank you

The artwork was prepared as collage constructions, which were reproduced in full color from photographs by Andrew Payne and David Blackwell.

The text type is Quorum Medium.

Copyright © 1995 by Jeannie Baker All rights reserved. No part of this book may be reproduced or utilized in any form or by any means, electronic or mechanical, including photocopying, recording, or by any information storage and retrieval system, without permission in writing from the Publisher, Greenwillow Books, a division of William Morrow & Company, Inc., 1350 Avenue of the Americas, New York, NY 10019. Printed in Singapore by Tien Wah Press First Edition
10 9 8 7 6 5 4 3 2 1

Library of Congress Cataloging-in-Publication Data
Baker, Jeannie.
The story of rosy dock / by Jeannie Baker.
  p.   cm.
ISBN 0-688-11491-1 (trade).   ISBN 0-688-11493-8 (lib. bdg.)
1. Rosy dock—Australia—Juvenile literature.   2. Natural History—Australia—Juvenile literature.   3. Plant introduction—Australia—Juvenile literature.   [1. Rosy dock.   2. Plant introduction—Australia.]   I. Title.   QK495.P78B34
1995   508.94—dc20   94-4677   CIP   AC

People say it is the oldest river in the world!
The Finke River begins in the center
of Australia, surrounded by desert and the
worn-down bones of prehistoric mountains.

For thousands of years
almost nothing here changed.

Then more than a hundred years ago
the first newcomers from Europe settled by the river.
With them they brought their animals . . .
horses and camels, cats, foxes, and rabbits.

Some years later another settler arrived.
She brought seeds from the other side of the world
and planted a garden.
One plant she especially loved for its beautiful red seedpods.

The land here is hot and dry.
Water is precious.

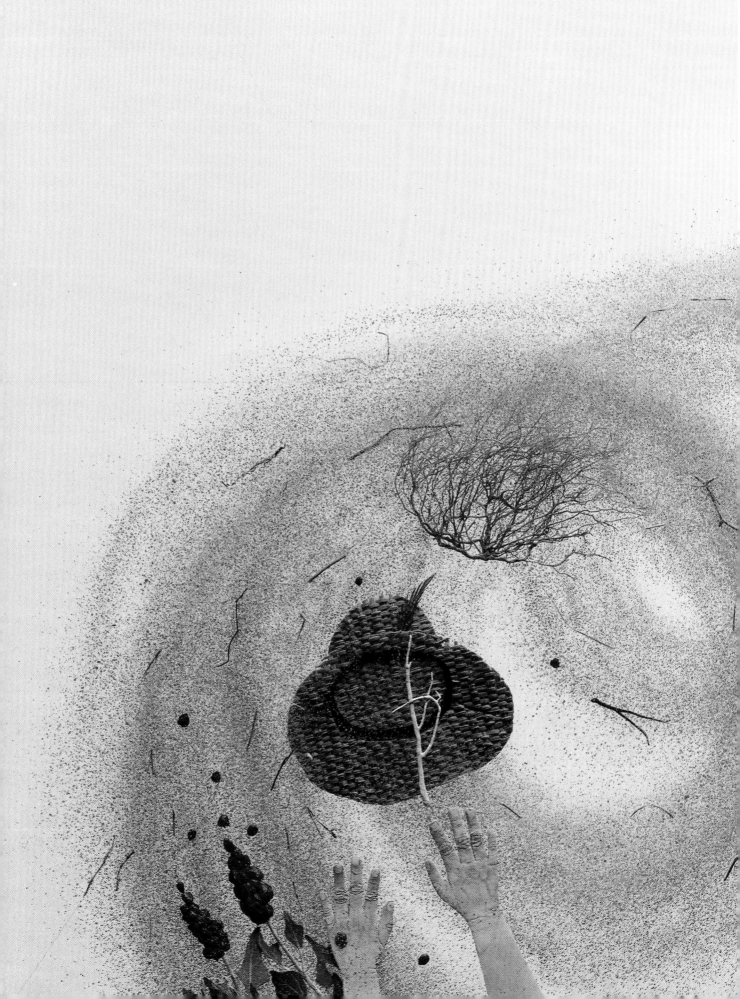

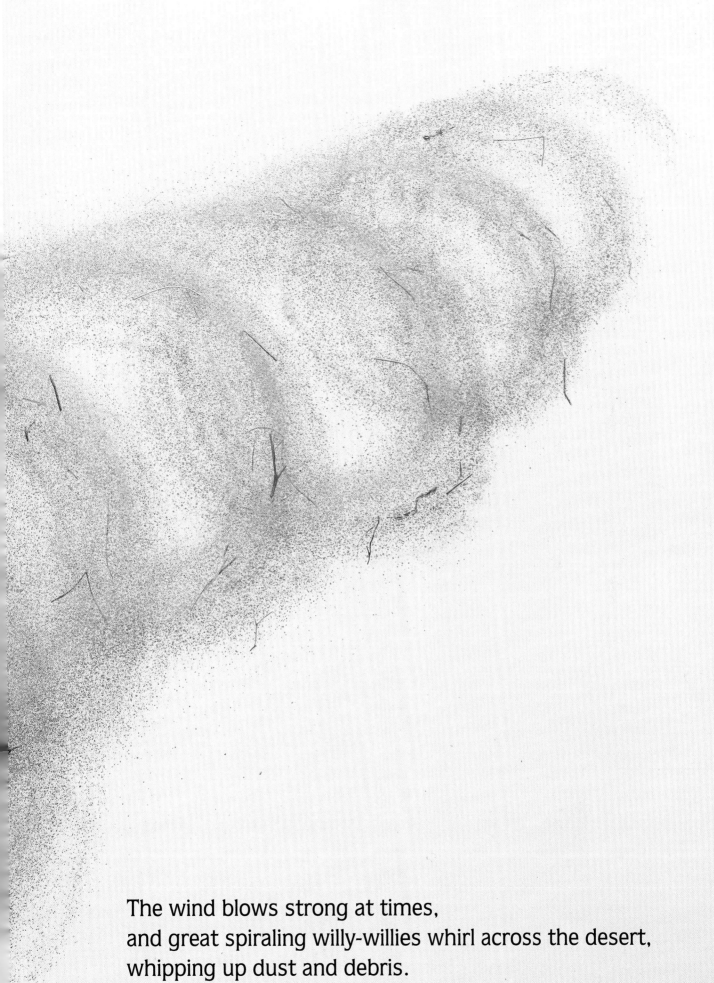

The wind blows strong at times,
and great spiraling willy-willies whirl across the desert,
whipping up dust and debris.

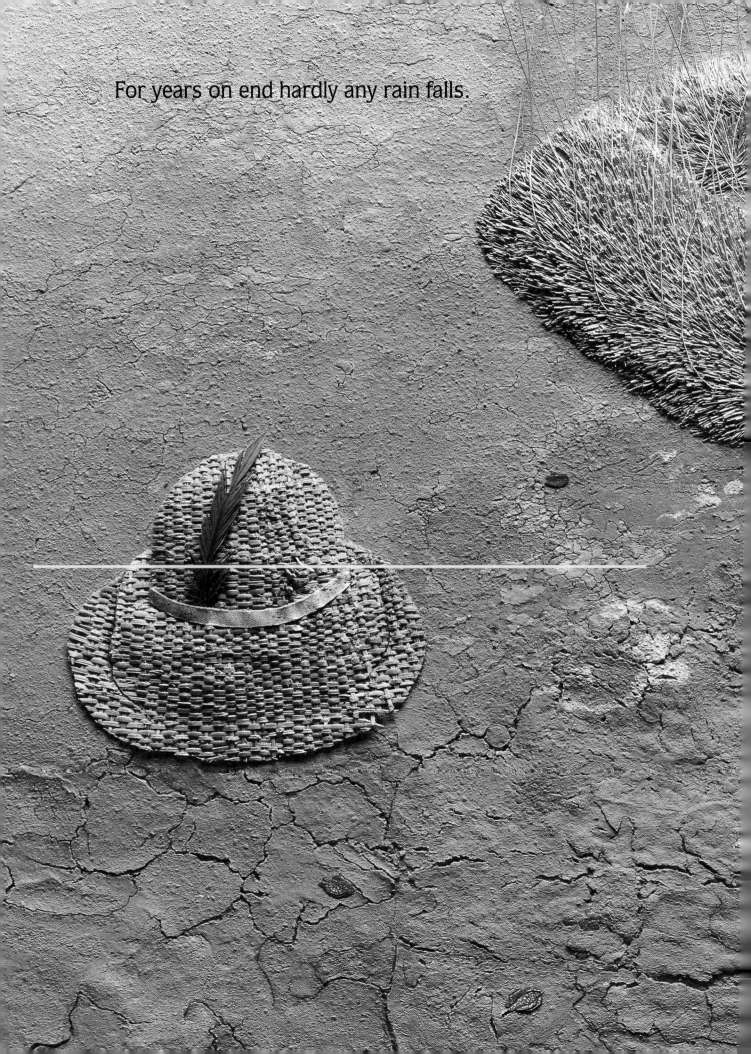

For years on end hardly any rain falls.

But hidden in the mountains
are ancient oases. Desert creatures
find water here even in the driest times.

The river is mostly a river of sand.

One day it was unnaturally dark, and there was an uneasy silence. Suddenly the sky cracked open.

Rain poured in torrents from the clouds,
and soon the river was roaring with water.

Rain kept pounding down,
and the river became a raging flood.

The flooded river swept on,
swirling, spiraling, surging on and on . . .

to a great sand-dune desert where it spread wide like a sea.

The water crept slowly across the desert
until it eventually disappeared into the sand.

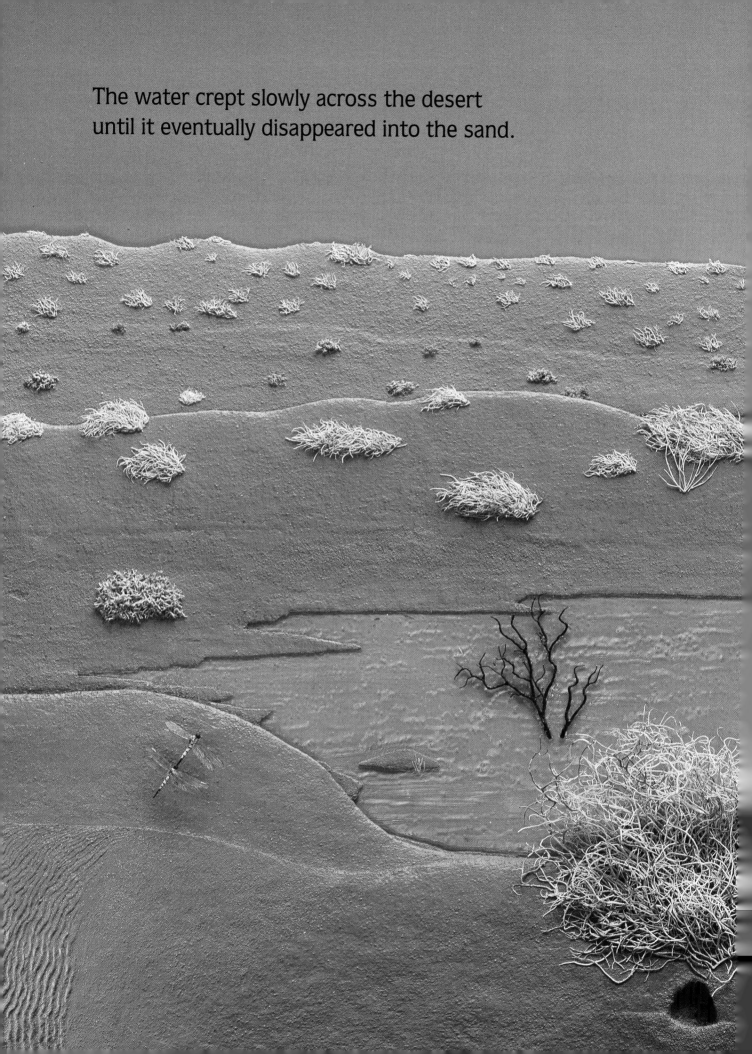

And then the desert
suddenly blossomed.
Birds and animals appeared.
The air came alive with insects,
and perfumed flowers
grew everywhere.

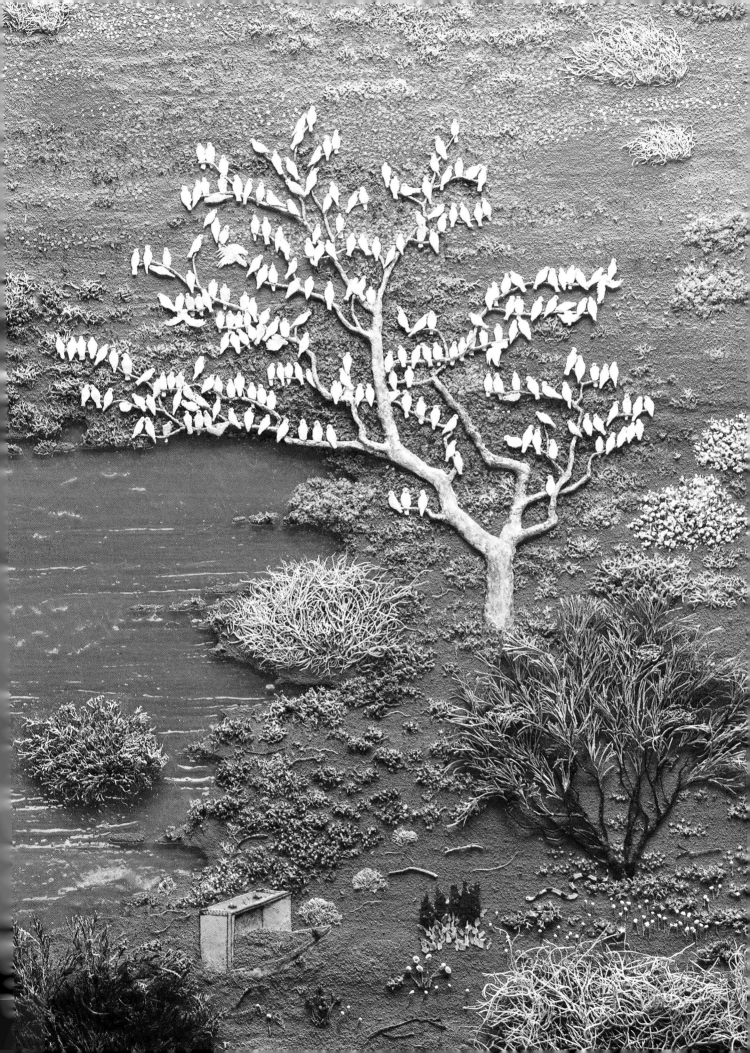

But the harsh, searing sun soon evaporated the water.
Winds sucked away the last traces of moisture,
leaving only mirage and a sea of rolling sand.

The pattern continues,
with many cycles of rain and drought.
Dust storms scatter seeds
and bury them in the desert sands.

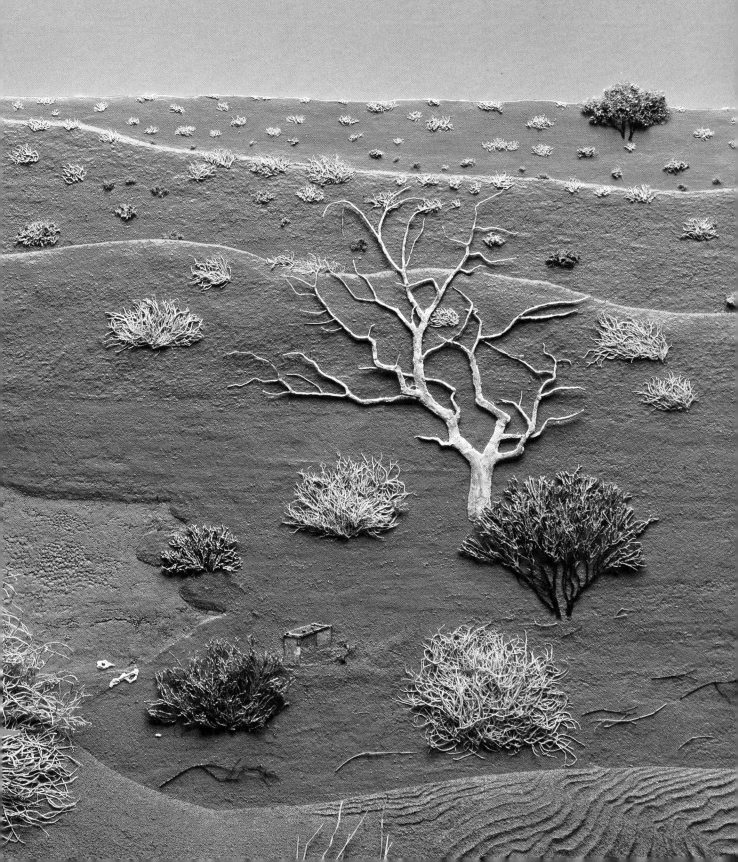

And now, after the rains have watered the desert,
rosy dock, the plant with beautiful red seedpods,
is spreading like a great red blanket
farther than the eye can see.

Rosy dock (*Rumex vesicarius*) is not native to Australia. It was introduced from North Africa or western Asia.
Since then seeds have blown their way across south, central, and western Australia, where rosy dock continues to spread.

Throughout the world, often with the best of intentions, people introduce plants and animals into a new environment with enormous unforeseen consequences. Without their normal predators, some non-native plants and animals multiply so quickly they change whole landscapes and push many native plants and animals to extinction.